Rescue Vehicles

An Hachette UK Company
www.hachette.co.uk

First published in Great Britain in 2012 by
TickTock, a division of Octopus Publishing Group Ltd
Endeavour House
189 Shaftesbury Avenue
London
WC2H 8JY
www.octopusbooks.co.uk

ISBN 978 1 84898 634 3

A CIP catalogue record for this book is available from the British Library

Printed and bound in China

10 9 8 7 6 5 4 3 2 1

Picture credits:
b=bottom; c=center; t=top; r=right; l=left
Alamy: p.9t, p.19t, p.26-27c. Bronto: p.1, p.6-7. Check–6 images: p.8-9c, p.14-15, p.26-27c. Jane's Defence Weekly: p.28-29c. London Fire Authority: p.19-20c. Oshkosh: p.4-5, p.10-11. Perry Slingsby Systems: p.24-25c. RNLI: p.20-21. Robinson Helicopters: p.12-13. Sylvia Corday Photo Library: p.25t. US Coastguard: p.2, p.16-17, p.22-23, p.29t.

Every effort has been made to trace the copyright holders, and we apologise in advance for any unintentional omissions. We would be pleased to insert the appropriate acknowledgments in any subsequent edition of this publication.

Contents

Striker 4500 Fire Engine

Charging from 0 to 80 km/h (50 mph) in 35 seconds, the Striker 4500 is the ultimate rapid emergency response vehicle. This giant fire engine is used to tackle airport fires. Costing around £615,000, a new model was introduced in 2010.

DID YOU KNOW?

The fire engine can spray foam because this is the quickest way to put out fuel fires.

Giant wheels give the Striker good grip when driving over muddy ground.

The 'snozzle' on the end of the fire engine's long arm can punch a hole in a plane and squirt foam on the fire inside.

LAUNCHED: 2002

ORIGIN: US

MAXIMUM POWER: 950 BHP

LENGTH: 13.6 M

WIDTH: 3.1 M

HEIGHT: 3.45 M

MAXIMUM SPEED: 112 KM/H (70 MPH)

CLEARANCE CIRCLE: 41 M

ACCELERATION: 0 TO 80 KM/H (50 MPH) IN 35 SECONDS

WATER TANK CAPACITY: 17,029 LITRES

FOAM TANK CAPACITY: 2,384 LITRES

MAXIMUM LOAD: 8.5 TONNES

WEIGHT: 52 TONNES

MEGA FACTOR: SPRAYS 4,750 LITRES A MINUTE

Firefighters get a good view of the scene. The cab features over 7.5 square metres of glass.

Bronto Skylift Fire Truck

The Bronto Skylift is designed to fight fires in tall buildings. It has the longest aerial platform in the world – it can reach to the 33rd floor of a building.

DID YOU KNOW?

This fire engine can shoot water or foam to extinguish fires.

The aerial platform can be controlled from the platform or the ground.

The highest aerial platforms offered on any model stretches to 112 metres.

A thick steel hose unfolds when the Skylift is called into action.

LAUNCHED: 2000

ORIGIN: FINLAND

MAXIMUM POWER: 480 BHP

LENGTH: 15 M

WIDTH: 2.5 M

TRUCK HEIGHT: 3.9 M

MAXIMUM SPEED: 64 KM/H (40 MPH)

FUEL CAPACITY: 265 LITRES

WATER DISCHARGE CAPACITY: 3,800 LITRES PER MINUTE

ROTATION: 360°

MAXIMUM LOAD: 400 KG

WEIGHT: 47.5 TONNES

CREW: 5

Heavy Rescue 56 Truck

This amazing vehicle is used by the Los Angeles Fire Department in all kinds of extreme situations. The Heavy Rescue 56 is called to accidents that involve everything from overturned lorries to collapsed buildings and crushed vehicles.

DID YOU KNOW?

Because of their specialised role, most heavy rescue vehicles don't have onboard water tanks or pumping gear.

The thick steel cable can lift an object that weighs as much as 15 cars. This is an essential feature in emergency situations.

Onboard equipment includes 'jaws of life', generators, cutting torches, cranes and circular saws.

In dangerous situations, the boom can be operated by remote control.

STATS & FACTS

LAUNCHED: 1995

ORIGIN: US

MAXIMUM POWER: 460 BHP

LENGTH: 10 M

WIDTH: 3 M

HEIGHT: 3.5 M

MAXIMUM SPEED: 160 KM/H (100 MPH)

FUEL CAPACITY: 299 LITRES

MAXIMUM LOAD: 36.2 TONNES

WEIGHT: 2.2 TONNES

GEARS: 18 FORWARD/4 REVERSE

CREW: 5

Medtec Saturn Ambulance

Ambulances rush to the scene of accidents and provide emergency treatment to casualties before taking them to the nearest hospital at high speed.

Some of the Saturn's life-saving equipment is electrically powered. The ambulance carries a battery pack to operate this machinery.

DID YOU KNOW?

The first ambulances were horse-drawn wagons. Motorised versions started to appear in the early 1900s.

Double rear doors make it easy to load stretchers into the ambulance.

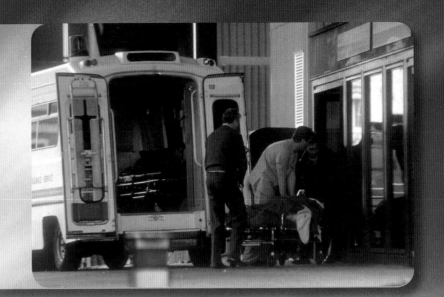

Flashing lights and sirens indicate that this is an emergency vehicle.

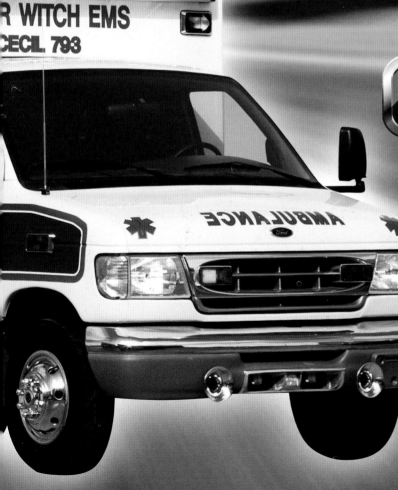

STATS & FACTS

LAUNCHED: 2000

ORIGIN: US

MAXIMUM POWER: 200 BHP

LENGTH: 4.2 M

WIDTH: 2.37 M

MAXIMUM SPEED: 122 KM (70 MPH)

FUEL CAPACITY: 208 LITRES

MAXIMUM LOAD: 2 TONNES

WEIGHT: 6 TONNES

CREW: 2

R44 Helicopter

This four-seater helicopter gives police forces a 'bird's-eye' view of action on the ground. It is loaded with special equipment, including an infrared imaging system, searchlight, monitor and dual audio controller for police radios.

Large windows provide a good view from all seats. Tinted windows and windscreens are also available.

DID YOU KNOW?

A special link lets the crew send live pictures to police on the ground.

The Robinson Helicopter Company was founded in 1973 by Frank Robinson. It also produces 'newscopters', which are used in the TV industry.

Helicopters don't carry much fuel, so they can't go far without stopping. The R44 can stay in the air for three hours when fully fuelled.

STATS & FACTS

LAUNCHED: 1993

ORIGIN: US

MAXIMUM POWER: 1,500 BHP

LENGTH OF HELICOPTER (INC ROTORS): 11.76 M

ROTOR LENGTH: 10 M

HEIGHT: 3.28 M

CRUISE SPEED: 208 KM/H (130 MPH)

FUEL CAPACITY: 116 LITRES

EMPTY WEIGHT: 681 KG

MAXIMUM FLYING HEIGHT: 4,267 M

RANGE: OVER 480 KM (300 MILES)

SPECIAL EQUIPMENT: SEARCH LIGHT, SIREN, SPEAKER, COLOUR AND INFRARED CAMERAS

CREW: 2

COST: STARTING AT £430,750 (2012 MODEL)

Super Huey Helicopter

The Super Huey was first used by the US Army to transport troops and cargo. The California Department of Forestry and Fire Protection bought and modified these helicopters and now uses them to fight wildfires.

These special 'choppers' are big and quick. They can deliver a ten-person fire crew wherever needed.

DID YOU KNOW?

'Huey' is a nickname that stuck. The original name of the helicopter was HU-1 Iroquois.

When the helicopter's water supply runs dry, the pilot can refill the tank at a lake or river. Water is sucked up through a hose.

The Super Huey can battle fires with either water or foam.

STATS & FACTS

LAUNCHED: 1990

ORIGIN: US

MAXIMUM POWER: 1,100 BHP

LENGTH: 17.32 M

ROTOR BLADE DIAMETER: 14.6 M

HEIGHT: 4.08 M

MAXIMUM SPEED: 223 KM/H (138 MPH)

CRUISE SPEED: 201 KM/H (126 MPH)

GROSS WEIGHT: 4.75 TONNES

RANGE: 400 KM

ENDURANCE: 2 HOURS

CREW: 1 PILOT, 2 FIRE CAPTAINS, 8 FIREFIGHTERS

P-3 Orion Firefighting Airtanker

P-3 Airtankers are old military aircraft that were originally developed as spy planes. They were adapted for civilian use and are now used to fight forest fires. They carry massive amounts of fire retardant, which is dropped on the blaze below.

DID YOU KNOW?

The Orion is named after a group of stars called Orion, the Great Hunter.

The P-3 used for firefighting has low wings and four turbine engines with four-blade propellers.

Computer-controlled doors under the body of the plane open to drop the retardant.

The fire retardant is dropped in a line, which acts as a barrier to stop the fire from spreading.

STATS & FACTS

LAUNCHED (AS AIRTANKER): 1990

ORIGIN: US

MAXIMUM POWER: 2,500 BHP

LENGTH: 35.6 M

WINGSPAN: NEARLY 30 M

HEIGHT: 11.8 M

MAXIMUM SPEED: 657 KM/H (411 MPH)

RETARDANT TANK CAPACITY:
11,356 LITRES

MAXIMUM LOAD: 20 TONNES

WEIGHT: 43.4 TONNES

MAXIMUM TAKEOFF WEIGHT:
63.4 TONNES

TAKEOFF RUN REQUIRED: 1,300 M

CREW: 15

Fire Dart Fireboat

The Fire Dart is a firefighting boat that patrols the River Thames in London. It is one of the lightest and quickest fireboats ever built.

DID YOU KNOW?

The Fire Dart can stop in about 14 metres.

A jet called a deck monitor shoots water in a stream over a fire. The rescue boat releases 1,800 litres per minute.

Fireboats and firefighting tugboats tackle fires on board ships. There is never a danger that they will run out of water because they take their water from the river or sea.

Two massive engines provide more than 700 bhp!

STATS & FACTS

LAUNCHED: 1999

ORIGIN: UK

MAXIMUM POWER: 2 X 365 BHP

LENGTH: 14.10 M

WIDTH: 4.2 M

HEIGHT: 3 M

MAXIMUM SPEED: 30 KNOTS (56 KM/H / 30 MPH)

FUEL CAPACITY: 4,000 LITRES

MAXIMUM LOAD: 1.2 TONNES

WEIGHT: 6.1 TONNES

RANGE: 160 KM (100 MILES)

CREW: 4 CREW, PLUS 5 FIREFIGHTERS

Atlantic 75 Lifeboat

The Atlantic 75 is a Rigid Inflatable Lifeboat (RIB) used to rescue people in trouble up to 80 km (50 miles) out to sea. It has a glass-reinforced plastic hull topped by an inflatable tube called a sponson. The latest version of this boat is the Atlantic 85 Lifeboat.

The hull and sponson are divided into compartments. If one section is pierced, the boat will not sink.

DID YOU KNOW?

If the boat capsizes, the crew inflates an airbag. The boat then turns the right way up in seconds.

The first rigid-hull inflatable lifeboat was designed by the British-based Royal National Lifeboat Institution in the early 1960s. These boats are now used worldwide.

The outboard motors are immersion-proofed so if the boat capsizes they are not damaged.

STATS & FACTS

LAUNCHED: 1992

ORIGIN: UK

MAXIMUM POWER: 2 X 70 BHP

LENGTH: 7.5 M

HEIGHT: 50 CM

MAXIMUM SPEED: 32 KNOTS (60 KM/H / 37 MPH)

FUEL CAPACITY: 181 LITRES

MAXIMUM LOAD: 500 KG

WEIGHT: 1.4 TONNES

ENDURANCE: 3 HOURS AT MAXIMUM SPEED

CREW: 3

HH-60J Jayhawk

Air-sea rescue helicopters are used to save people stranded at sea. The HH-60J Jayhawk is employed by the US Coast Guard. In 2015, all 42 HH-60J helicopters will be updated. The new aircraft will be renamed the MH-60T.

DID YOU KNOW?

The Jayhawk is based on the VS-300 helicopter, developed by Russian-born American engineer Igor Sikorsky. The VS-300 first flew in 1939.

A satellite navigation system is used to find people in need of help. The pilot holds the helicopter in place while a rescuer is lowered by winch.

The small tail rotor stops the helicopter from spinning around and keeps it perfectly balanced.

STATS & FACTS

LAUNCHED: 1986

ORIGIN: US

MAXIMUM POWER: 2 X 1,800 BHP

LENGTH: 19.81 M

ROTOR DIAMETER: 16.46 M

HEIGHT: 5.18 M

CRUISE SPEED: 258 KM/H

MAXIMUM SPEED: 483 KM/H (300 MPH)

FUEL CAPACITY: 2,233 LITRES

MAXIMUM LOAD: 3.4 TONNES

WEIGHT: 6.1 TONNES

RANGE: 1,127 KM (700 MILES)

SURVIVOR CAPACITY: 6

CREW: 4

The rotor blades can be folded if the helicopter needs to be stored or transported.

LR7 Rescue Submersible

Perry Slingsby Systems is one of the world's leading makers of rescue submersibles. These machines help rescue passengers of submarines in distress. The LR7 replaced the earlier LR5.

The rear rescue chamber holds 18 evacuees, plus crew members.

DID YOU KNOW?

The LR7 is equipped with sonar. Sonar uses sound waves to guide the crew in the dark waters of the deep ocean.

In 2001, the LR5 was used in the attempt to free the crew of the Russian submarine *Kursk*. Unfortunately, the LR5 arrived too late to rescue the sailors.

A special section called a transfer skirt is attached to the escape hatch. Trapped passengers can then move safely to the LR7.

STATS & FACTS

LAUNCHED: 2004

ORIGIN: UK

MAXIMUM POWER: 10 BHP

LENGTH: 9.6 M

WIDTH: 3.2 M

HEIGHT: 3.4 M

MAXIMUM SPEED: 3 KNOTS
(5.6 KM/H / 3.5 MPH)

BATTERY CAPACITY: 144 LEAD
ACID BATTERIES

MAXIMUM LOAD: 2.75 TONNES

WEIGHT: 26.5 TONNES

RESCUE CAPACITY: 18 PEOPLE,
PLUS 2 PILOTS AND 1 MEDIC

Hagglunds BV206

The Hagglunds BV206 all-terrain vehicle is used for everything from firefighting to arctic rescue and disaster relief. This amazing vehicle even floats, which allows it to travel over thin ice.

Because it is light on its tracks, the Hagglunds BV206 can operate in snow, ice, mud, water, grass or sand.

DID YOU KNOW?

The BV206 is also used for desert exploration, jungle exploration and even as a snow taxi for tourists.

The all-terrain vehicle pictured is used to rescue people trapped in blizzards and snowdrifts. A special attachment pushes snow out of the way.

The rear car can be converted into an ambulance or even into a troop carrier in a matter of minutes.

STATS & FACTS

LAUNCHED: 1994

ORIGIN: SWEDEN

MAXIMUM POWER: 136 BHP

LENGTH: 7 M

WIDTH: 1.98 M

HEIGHT: 2.4 M

MAXIMUM SPEED: 51.5 KM/H (32 MPH) ON ROADS OR 3 KM/H (2 MP/H) IN WATER

FUEL CAPACITY: 90 LITRES

MAXIMUM LOAD: 2.5 TONNES

WEIGHT: 4.47 TONNES

CREW: 2

RESCUE CAPACITY: 10

Marine Protector

This is a Marine Protector Class US Coast Guard patrol boat. It is a fast, strong boat that can operate in rough seas. It is used to stop drug smugglers and chase other criminals. It is also used for search and rescue missions.

The pilot house is equipped with satellite navigation and autopilot.

DID YOU KNOW?

Each of the 73 boats in the US Coast Guard fleet is named after a marine predator. Names include *Marlin*, *Stingray* and *Mako*.

U.S. COAST GUARD

A small diesel-powered boat is kept at the back of the patrol boat. It is launched and recovered on a specially designed ramp. Only one person is required on deck for launch and recovery.

In America and the UK this boat is called a cutter. Cutters are boats that are more than 20 metres long.

STATS & FACTS

LAUNCHED: 1998

ORIGIN: US

MAXIMUM POWER: 5,360 BHP

LENGTH: 26.5 M

WIDTH: 5.18 M

MAXIMUM SPEED: 25 KNOTS (45 KM/H / 28 MPH)

FUEL CAPACITY: 11,000 LITRES

MAXIMUM WEIGHT: 92.4 TONNES

TOWING CAPABILITY: 200 TONNES

SURVIVOR CAPACITY: 10

RANGE: 1,445 KM (900 MILES)

ENDURANCE: 5 DAYS

CREW: 10

Glossary

AERIAL PLATFORM Platform mounted on the end of a crane's arm.

ARM See boom.

AUTOPILOT System that operates a vehicle without a pilot.

BATTERY PACK A portable container that provides the electrical power to make things work.

BHP Brake horse power, the measure of an engine's power output.

BODY Main part of a vehicle that houses the driver and passengers.

BOOM A crane's long, extending arm.

CAB The part of a truck or digger that houses the driver and controls.

CABIN A room in a ship used as living quarters by an officer or passenger, or the part of a plane that houses the pilot and passengers.

CAPSIZE When a boat turns over in the water.

CASUALTY An injured or sick person.

COCKPIT The part of an aircraft where the pilot and his assistants sit.

CRANE A machine for lifting by means of cables attached to a boom.

CUTTER A boat more than 20 m (65 feet) long.

DECK MONITOR Water jet on a fireboat that shoots water high into the air.

ENGINE The part of a vehicle where fuel is burned to create energy.

FIRE RETARDANT Liquid dropped onto fires to stop them from spreading.

FOAM Frothy substance used to fight fires.

HOSE A tube that carries pressured liquids or gases.

HULL The lower part of a boat.

IMMERSION-PROOFED Protected from water damage.

INFLATABLE A small rubber boat or raft filled with air.

INFRARED CAMERA A camera that can record images at night.

KNOT One nautical mile per hour, equal to 1.85 kilometres per hour or 1.15 miles per hour.

MONITOR A mounted water cannon that throws powerful jets of water at a fire.

NOZZLE The end of a hose. Different nozzle attachments result in a different type of water spray, from a mist to a continuous stream.

PILOT HOUSE Part of a ship where the pilot and the controls are based.

PROPELLER A machine with spinning blades that lifts an aircraft off the ground.

PUMP A machine that raises or lifts a liquid or gas.

REMOTE CONTROL The control of an object from a distance.

RIGID HULL INFLATABLE BOAT Boat with a plastic hull topped by an inflatable tube called a sponson.

ROTOR Spinning blade.

SATELLITE NAVIGATION A system that tells you where you are, using satellites in space.

SONAR A system that uses underwater sound waves to detect and locate objects or measure distances.

SPONSON An air-filled tube that helps stabilise a boat on the water.

SUBMERSIBLE A boat that can function under water.

SUBMARINE See submersible.

TANK A large container used to store fuel.

TRACKS Two flexible metal loops that help a vehicle grip on muddy or icy ground.

TUG A powerful boat that pulls or pushes ships.

TURBINE Machine with a wheel or rotor driven by water, steam or gases.

WINCH The method of lifting something by winding a line around a spool.

WINGSPAN The distance between the tips of the wings of an aircraft.

Index